First, I found
my words with a pen
in between the lines of pages,
and I realized how much I had to say,
so I dug up the voice I buried long ago
to speak them

What are memories of childhood
if not quicksand?
Swallowing you whole.

The outside of my house is perfect.
The outer walls are painted in
a bright green colour.
The plants that circle its perimeter
are lush with life and vibrancy.
The roof is sloped, yet stable.

The atmosphere it encompasses
is beautiful.

The inside of my house is damaged.
The inner walls are painted
white and hide secrets
beneath their chipped paint.

The staircase creaks in the right places
to alert those either below or above.

The dining room table
is suitable for eight
but never seats one.

The stained-glass window
features a crack
from an object that was not meant to hit it.

The atmosphere it encompasses
is suffocating with secrets.

Outer eyes see its perfection.
Inner eyes see its destruction.

Childhood is brief
and mine was cut shorter.

An older sister is a mother
when mom can't be home
too busy working,
working, working to the grave for us.

But then I learned
what mom's crying looked like,
learned homework over his yelling,
to keep my pencil steady
as I filled out a multiplication table
despite the tremble of my hand

and that red and blue lights
flashing outside your house at night
can be as common as the stars
when you have a cruel man inside it,
too in love with his bottles.

All these things a child should never learn,
so I learned then to stop being a child.

The problem
with being
brought up
a good christian girl

you learn it's normal
to love a man
who can't say
he loves you
back.

That flicker in his eyes,
the one you thought was love,
turned out to be hell and chaos.

From your lips. To your throat.
To your stomach. To your head.
To your words. To your fists.

That is the path the liquid
takes every night.

When you drink it, it makes you powerful.
When you drink it, it makes you angry.

When you drink it, it makes you forget.

When you drink it, it makes me weak.
When you drink it, it makes me empty.

When you drink it, I'll never forget.

You should
never love
anything
more than
you love
your own children.

You should
never love
anyone
more than
you love
your own children.

- How could you?

I am afraid of love
because I have seen
what it has done
to my mother.

It must be so hard
to love the ones
who are
half of him.

My father made
so many mistakes
but he is just human.

How can I not
keep forgiving
the man who is half of

my word weaving brain,

my belief that anything is possible,

my uncontrollable need to be near water.

I saw vulnerability
drip from
my father's eyes
for the first time
when I was twelve.

I learned the
sweet sick balance of
empathy and blame.

Empathy tugs lightly on my sleeve
and gently whispers in my ear,
"they are struggling too".

I counted fourteen days
on the calendar in our kitchen.

Two trips to the grocery store.
Two loads of laundry.
Fourteen walks with the dogs.
Nine times the sun woke me up.

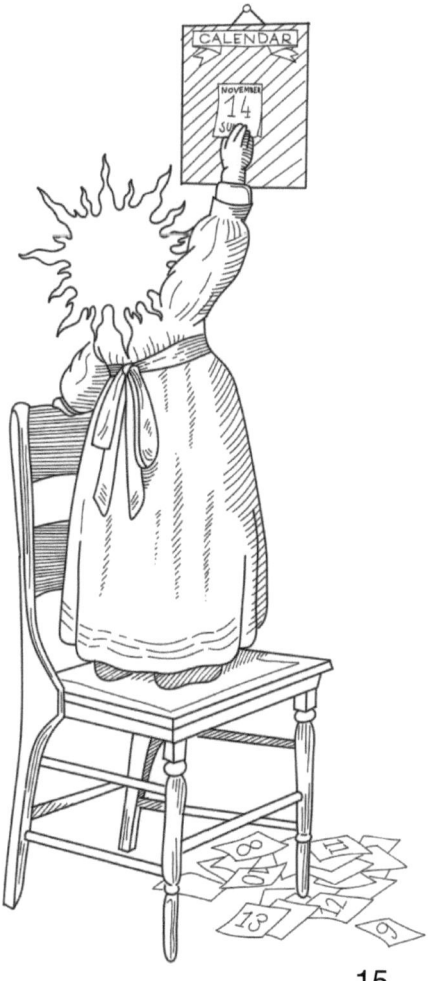

Four rainy days
stuck in a house
that was not a
home.

I crossed off the
fourteenth day
on the calendar,
and went
downstairs
to read my
siblings
a book before
bed.

Where are you?

My biggest secret
is the broken house
I know as a home.

My biggest secret
is the destruction
that lies within it.

I don't let the suffocating
secrets slip out of the cracks.

I keep them buried.
I am prepared to keep them
buried for the rest of my life.

My friends think
I am busy on the weekends.

My teachers think
I got lazy with my assignments.

My siblings think
I am their parent.

I think
I am a kid.

You fear the violence
they might do
if you let them
know your secrets.

- Maybe that's why you push them away.

I want you to know me.
I want to pour light into
the pitch black caves
that hide my secrets.

In my mind's eye
I always see you
sitting by yourself
at the kitchen table,

smoking your cigarette,
drinking your coffee
and wanting to be
anywhere else
but here with me.

The last time I felt my mother's love
was when I was in her womb.

She spent nine months
delicately curating me.

My eyes.
My heart.

When she laid her eyes on me
for the first time,
she realized she could never love me.

My eyes saw through her.
My heart followed a different beat.

She discarded me the day
she laid her eyes on me.

I was made with love.
I was not made to be loved.

My mother's love
became a knife
lodged in my back.
I could never decide between
letting it stay
and living with the pain
or removing it
and bleeding to death.

My mother is an artist too.
Somehow, somewhere along the way,

I forgot that we artists
have some creations
that we don't like.

The realization came late,
almost like everything else in my life.

I am torn between anger and empathy.

The nights when you abandoned me,
I was angry for feeling your neglect.

Yet I understood you wanted to feel loved.

The days when you
closed the door to parenting,
I was angry for feeling your distance.

Yet I understood you never had a parent.

I am angry because
I wanted to feel loved.
I am angry because
I wanted to have a parent.

Yet I understand
I was too hard to love.
Yet I understand
I was too much of a burden.

And I can't even look back in anger,
my mother loved me before she didn't,
which means the mistake
must have been me.

I just think
some women
aren't made to be
mothers

and some women
aren't made to
be daughters.

I'm sorry
if I wasn't
the daughter
you had in mind.

There are some mothers
who will warn you

to never ever
touch the stove,

but there are some mothers
who will drag you right to it

kicking and screaming,
laughing as they

watch the flames
lick at your fingertips.

I have searched
for my mother's love
in all corners of the world.

There was never
enough alcohol
to keep me warm
in a house
as cold
as this.

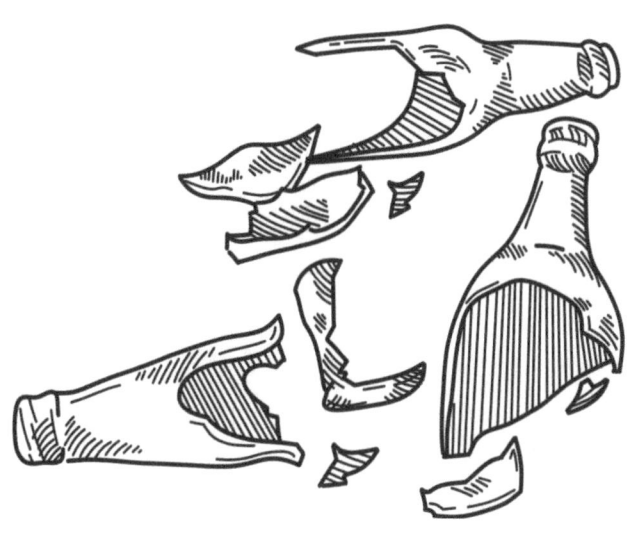

To love is tender?
I am trying to learn
that it is gentle,
trying to forget
what I have known.

What my mother learned
from her mother.

Cycle building.

My heart grew up
to be far more starved
than my stomach.

It's the things you learn
in your childhood.

From the words your mother.
From the hands of your father.

To forgive and forget,
how perfect would that be?

If I stopped believing in ghosts,
would the hauntings go away?

There are so many things
I am dying to un-live and unlearn,

but how could I possibly forget
what I still feel in my bones?

I swear,
some memories have a way

of permanently feeling
like they happened today.

That is what abuse is:
knowing you are going to get salt
but still hoping for sugar
for nineteen years.

- I still have a stomachache.

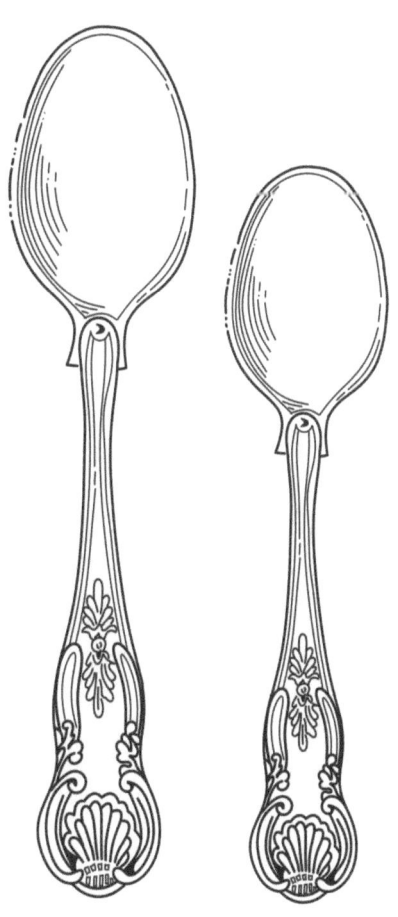

I have my father's nose
and all his rage.
I have my mother's face
and her grief.

Rage, I have learned to wear.
My mother's grief, however,
folds my spine and
lives beneath my ribs.

It gets heavier and heavier.

You had scars from your mother.
Burrowed under your skin.
Neglect passed down to you.

I have scars from my mother.
Burrowed under my skin.
Neglect passed down to me.

My daughter will not
have scars from her mother.
They will not be burrowed under her skin.
Neglect will not be passed down to her.

I will break the cycle.

At eleven years old
the doctor weighed me
and afterward,
my mother told me
I was too fat
and that I needed to go
on a diet immediately.

For an entire year,
food barely passed
through my lips.

I didn't even allow myself
to take a sip of water
because I wanted to be
so thin that I
could blow away
with the slightest breeze.

Fat kid,
don't sit on my lap.

Kid why don't
you wear jeans.

Kid those sweatpants
make you look fat.

Kid you're going to eat
another one.

Kid you finished
the whole bag.

Kid why are
you crying kid,

it's time to thicken
your fat skin.

Sticks and stones
never broke
my bones,
but words
made me
starve myself
until
you could
see all of them.

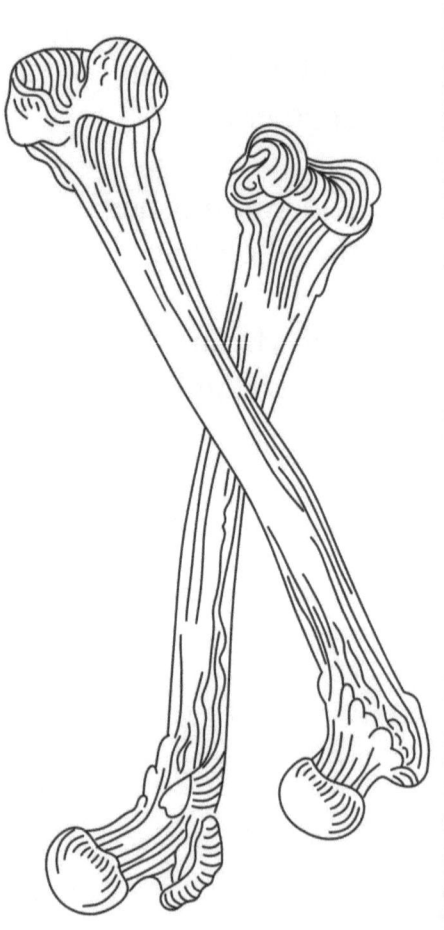

Just because
they don't hit you
doesn't mean it
isn't abuse.

Wouldn't you think
it's a crime
to look up
at the night sky
and tell the stars
that they have
no sparkle?

Guess what?
You shine brighter
than all the starlight
there has ever been
or ever will be.

- Emotional abuse is still abuse.

I figured if I held
my breath long enough

and sucked my stomach up
under my ribs far enough

and powdered my face pale enough
and gave myself enough razor burns
and plucked the hairs between my eyebrows
until my eyes watered

and painted my nails girly enough
and squeezed my jeans on tight enough
and demolished my natural beauty enough

I'd be pretty enough.

I would like to eat
even just one meal
without feeling
ashamed.

I tried to starve myself into thin.
I felt faint on the school's track
and I slept with a waist trainer,
cramming my stomach away,
strangling my intestines out of order,
so I could fulfill their idea
of what beauty is.

But it was ugly,
a tainted wish-
Starvation, judgment,
making an enemy
of my body
and my soul's
sacred home.

I am tired of trying to love you.
I get why it is so hard
for others to do the same.

I cannot keep you around me.
I want you out of my body.
you eat me from the inside.
I am sick with your sadness.

My home has a heart.

My home has lungs.

My home has a brain.

My home has 206 bones.

My home heals me
when my heart breaks.

My home heals me
when my chest feels tight.

My home heals me
when my brain works against me.

My home heals me
when I physically break.

My home doesn't love me.

If you ever look
at your reflection
and feel the desire
to tell yourself
you're not
good enough,
beautiful enough,
skinny enough,
curvy enough,

then I think
it's about time
you smashed
that mirror to bits,
don't you?

I'm hungry
but I have no appetite
it's hard to be
when you have this feeling
inside your stomach
eating you out from within.

How I spend my days today
isn't how I'll spend my days forever.
Knowing this gives me hope.

- Someday, it will get better.

The hatred for the
word mother is so sweet.

You can hate
everything related to it:
Mother tongue,
Mother's hometown,
Motherhood, everything.

But then you say mom
and you're six years old again,
standing at
the foot of
her bed,
waiting for
her to open
the covers,
let you in
and ask you
about your
misery.

You know,
before she
became a
part of it.

I am a tall child
with no lap to crawl into
and cry in.

So I make a big show
of wounded skin,
hoping someone pries in.

Shame clots in my blood.
I am humiliated, just by existing.

You remember too much,
my mother said to me recently.
Why hold onto all that?

And I said, where can I put it down?

Is there a home for me somewhere?

There's always
a home.
The one you're
running to
or the one
you're running
from.

People aren't homes,
they never will be.

People are rivers,
always changing,
forever flowing.

They will disappear
with everything
you put inside them.

You may
not have left
(many) bruises
on my skin,
but you left
blueberries
all over my soul.

There is not
enough rainwater
in all the skies
to rinse the
innocent blood
from your hands.

My mother says
there are locked rooms
inside all women;

kitchen of lust,
bedroom of grief,
bathroom of apathy.

Sometimes, the men
they come with keys,
and sometimes, the men
they come with hammers.

My first kiss:
tackled, pinned down,
a mouth repeating
no no no.

After:
bruises and the unmistakable
taste of blood.

- I will never forgive you.

Yes.
I mean, no.
I mean, maybe.
I mean, is it really
lying to myself
if I say I wanted it?

That he loved me?

When he tells me
I am good when I am quiet,
I resist the impulse
to cry under his body.

I definitely wanted it
because he said
I was the prettiest
at the party.

I kissed him first
and he pushed too far.

It turns out,
even monsters feel desire.

I only wanted to be needed.

If my bruises swell up
I'll have a bigger part
of your love.

What happens
under the blankets
can either be
pure magic
or pure barbarity

and when the latter
is reported,
it is time and time
again mistaken
for the former.

When you are telling your truth,
do not let anyone minimize it.

Do not let them tell you it is wrong.
Do not let them tell you
it did not happen that way.

Do not let them tell you it does not hurt.
If you felt it was right,
don't let them tell you it was wrong.

If you felt it happened a certain way,
don't let them tell you it did not.

If you felt hurt,
don't let them tell you you're not.

What you experienced is your truth.
No one can take that away from you.

Repeat after me:
you owe no one
your forgiveness.

- Except maybe yourself.

You did
absolutely nothing
to deserve it.

I'm locked out of my home.
No, I can't recognize my home.

I grabbed the wrong keys.

The house has been painted
a different color.

There is music inside
but I don't understand the words.

There is smoke inside,
but nothing was burning.

I cried -
not because of the
house
but because of the
memories
that already lie
inside it
and the ones
that I could still
have had.

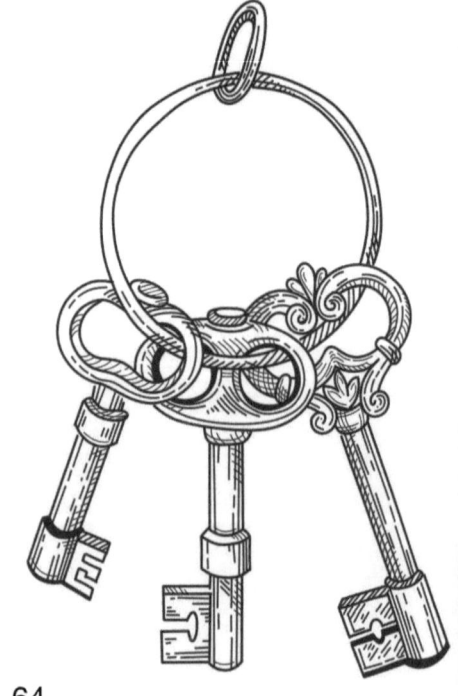

But mostly,
I grieve for the girl
I could have been.

And the woman
I would have been
if his touch
never marked
my skin.

The love
some girls have
for other girls
is so gentle
and so soft
and so beautiful.

These girls
deserve to have better stories
than the ones,
where they are murdered
because they love
with too much
of their hearts.

- Love is never a weakness.

You are not what happened to you.
You are so much more than that.

You are a multitude of
stories and journeys
that have shaped you to be you.

But they have done just that.
And only that.

Shaped you.
They are not you.

You are more than
what happened to you.

If people can hate for no reason
I can love for no reason.

Lies flow from your lips
thick like honey
so sweet that
I forget to think twice
before blindly believing
the words you feed me.

Spite
and offering to others
what has been promised to another.

Wondering why you aren't enough
and cutting words
chopping you smaller.

Tears and doubts
yelling and slammed doors.

Bruised skin, dented refrigerators
a house now a place of war.

This is everything love is not.
Please don't fall for a liar's charms.

Learn lessons from all you've seen
and remember:
Love isn't meant to cause harm.

Hope is what leads
to disappointment,
yet I still can't stop hoping
for a life of happiness
together with you.

And that shocks me,
because minutes
before we had met,
I was entirely convinced
that I would never
hope in anything ever again.

If it doesn't hurt it isn't love
I saw this quote once and thought
that was how love is supposed to be.

- I couldn't be more wrong.

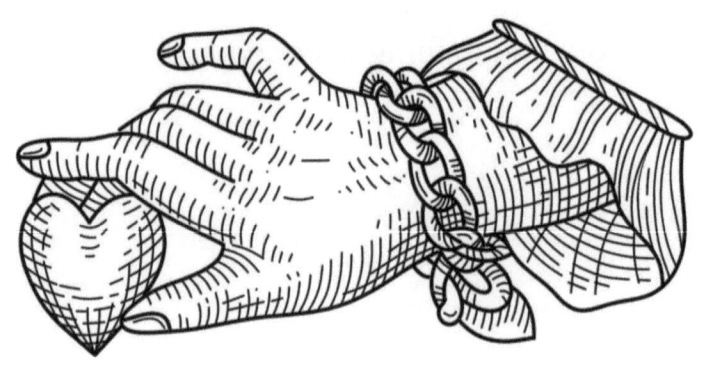

Sometimes
(the best times)
love comes in like a
break in the rain.

It's the thing we
didn't expect but had,
in the back of our minds,
hoped would happen.

We keep a little hope
somewhere in us that,
someday, someone
will come along and
make the sunlight come back.

I was lost in this world,
wandering blindly with
a heart so broken
I could see no point
in even trying to put it back together.

But then I found you,
and that no longer seemed
to make any sense to me.

And in the process of falling
madly, wildly, incomparably hard for you,

I found a reason to take those pieces
and put them all back where they belonged.

The first time we met
was a wednesday afternoon.

I can't remember
the rest of the details
because I never thought
you would become
an important person to me.

I wonder what
would happen
if you knew,
that since you
first kissed me,
my lips have
not stopped
asking for you.

He opened me up
like a book
and poured
the poetry
back into me.

- My personal pen and paper.

And every day,
I will love you
like a poet,
where every
little detail
never goes
unnoticed.

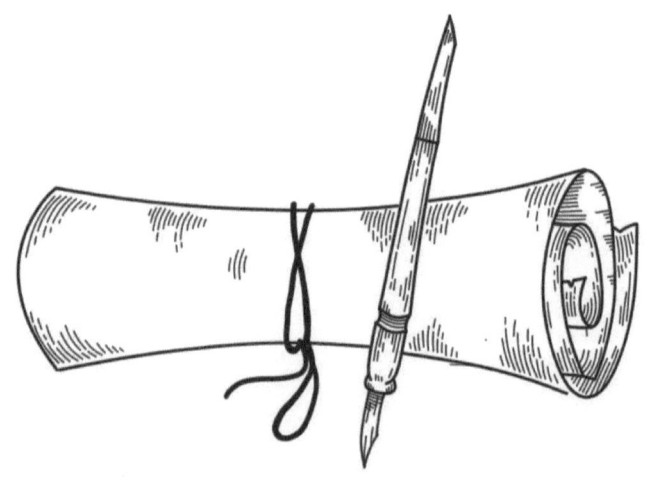

I am a slave to whatever 'love' is.
Hot, heavy, uncomfortable love,
it has dug its nails into me
and I am pleading for it to dig deeper.
Yes.
Yes!
Take a hold of me,
drive yourself into me
and split me straight
down the middle.
Leave me in pieces,
oh ruin me,
love,
ruin me!

I can't explain where
all my love for you
came from.

It's as if we once raised a child,
baby fingers gripping pinkies
or died together on a bed of daisies.

It's as if I were the sun
and you were the moon.
Always convincing each other
the next day was worth rising for.

And when I was too caught up
in being the ocean
you never forgot to remind me
what it feels like to burn.

I can't believe we finally
collided in this century
because I am certain
I have loved you
in more than a thousand
different lifetimes.

I am a poet
and I think the moon
is your metaphor.

I sit by the sun, burning,
as we both admire.

There's something
about you, me,
and moonlight
through an open window
that makes me forget
that anything bad
has ever happened
in my past.

If I could heal your wounds, I would.
If I could replace your suffering, I would.
If I could bottle up your pain, I would.

Seeing you wounded is the worst pain.
Seeing you suffering is the worst ache.
Seeing you bottle up your pain
is the worst sorrow.

I would take it from you any day.

I would care for you how
I wished you cared for me.

My mother remembers
the blanket I had as a child
that went everywhere with me
until I tossed it out of a moving car,
unaware that it wouldn't return.

God please,
I worry I'd be given love
without knowing where to put it.

What if I toss it away
and spend the rest of my life
thinking about it?

I don't know
how to talk about love
without talking about violence.

Darling,
I destroy everything I love.

Like my favourite cup
that I held a little too tightly
because I was afraid
that it would fall
and break into pieces.

It shattered in my hands.

Please don't
leave me.

I thought
I would have a lifetime
to be in love with you.

It ended in a second.

If it was meant to be
we would still be
together.

How many times
can you say goodbye
to a person
before you finally
leave them?

I missed the train again

and I called your name
as if you'd drive it back

I miss you so.

Long train ride
journey home alone.
It's a little cold tonight
but I'll be alright.

Phone lights up,
wrong notification.
Maybe tonight isn't the night
but I'll be alright.

It's almost 4am,
can't sleep, can't stop thinking.
Gotta get up in 2 hours
but I'll be alright.

Brand new day
still stuck on yesterday.
Probably another cycle tonight
but I'll be alright.

Does it say more
about me or you?

If I told you
that I am still here,
waiting,
to do all the things
we said we would do.

So much of me went with you.
One heart beats for two.

Your heart used to beat for me too.

The war is over;
the bombs have all
been dropped.

Most people would
say I've won,
yet here I lie
months later
feeling
defeated.

- Soulmates, huh?

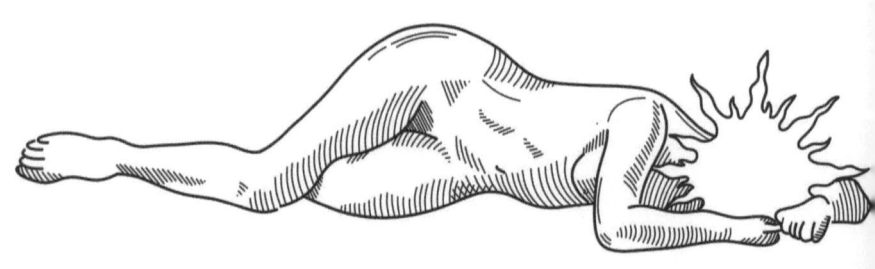

"I will be alone this winter.
Sorry if I gave you the wrong impression
but my heart isn't warm enough
to keep either of us alive."

You won't have to convince
your soulmate to stay.

You made me feel new things
when I was convinced I'd felt it all.

Why should I ever
look back in anger at that?

Even when I'm 70,
I'd still remember
how my heart
loved you at 17.

You and I
together again
will always be
something
I think about.

It would break my heart in two
when you'd make my pain about you.

- You weren't why I suffered.

What is a confession of love
if not the original apology?
I love you.
I am sorry.

Sometimes,
I wonder if you'd
love this person
I've become,
or if you'd
leave the new me too?

The birds sing in the evening too.
Did they always do that?

I never noticed before now.

How many
funerals can
someone attend
before they turn nineteen?

Why did the stars
need you more than I did?

I was a child.

If your best friend is dead,
is she still your best friend?

Or is she something else?
If someone you've never met dies,
did they ever really exist?

Minutes before
your mother
made the
death call,
I smelled your
warm vanilla perfume
and my mouth
filled with the taste
of dirt.

- Death is one of the senses.

I was the one
who found your body.

Mouth opened
wide enough
to suck all the oxygen
from the room,

wide enough
to plant
sunflowers in,
wide enough
to have been
calling my name.

- I want to forget,
  forget, forget.

Sometimes I think about
what I would have done
if I had known
we had such a short
amount of time left together.

I wish I'd hugged you
a little more often.

- My deepest regret.

How strange
that the
world can
just carry on
without you.

When you took your last breath,
I forgot how to breathe.

When you closed your eyes
for the last time,
my vision became clouded.

When your voice was
no longer heard,
I forgot how to speak.

When you died,
a piece of me died with you.

The world stopped turning
the day you died.

I felt it.
In my bones.
In my heart.
In every fibre of my being.
I felt it.

The sun stopped being warm.
The night stopped being cool.
The birds no longer sang.

When you died,
the world as I knew it did too.

I did too.

The last time
I felt sunshine on my face
was when you were alive.

It was warm.
It filled me with joy.
It made me loathe rainy days.

Now you are gone,
and the sun burns me.

It is cold.
It fills me with sorrow.
It makes me wish for rainy days.

It's in the dying light of the day
when I'm reminded of your face
and all the ways I lost you.

I resented the world
for continuing to exist without you.

I resented the world
for forcing me to exist without you.

The day your soul left this earth,
was the day mine did too.

My heart no longer beats the
same.

My eyes no longer see the same.

My mind no longer thinks the same.

While I am physically here,
my soul is with yours.

Bound together in the rays of the sun.

Every poem is a letter I'll never send,
this pen is running out of ink
and I'm not finished
writing you out of the story yet -
you'll never really leave, will you?

There's a storm in my veins
and it clamors
everytime I hear your name.

You haunt my body,

I'm becoming fragile
getting you out of my system
and am growing tired holding on.

I don't even have a life, anymore.
I just sit in my backyard, smoke
and wonder where you are.

If I had the entire world
resting on one of my fingertips,

I'd blow it away
like a dandelion
and wish that all of us
could just start over
and try again,

make a world full of love
instead of this tragic
kind of madness
we have today.

I wish time was kind to you.

There is so much I wanted to tell you.

So much I wish I said.

Now I tell it to the moon,
hoping you're there.

In another universe,
it would have been me instead of you.

In this universe,
I would have chosen me instead of you.

I wish it was me.

I am caught
between
mourning you
and thinking
your death
saved me.

I'm tired of grieving.

I'm tired of wishing I could sleep
my days away,
as that is the only time I see you.

I'm tired of living through photos
in my camera roll,
as that is the only time I see you.

I'm tired of grasping at memories,
as that is the only time I see you.

I'm tired of living with grief,
instead of you.

Why am I still here,
did I survive
or was I left behind?

Months after my best friend died,
I found the book she was reading
with a yellowing receipt
still tucked inside,
marking her place,
and it finally hit me.

You will never get to finish
this particular book.

You will never get to start
or finish another book ever again.

You will never
meet the love of my life.

You will never
be there for my wedding.

You will never
read these words.

We will never
ever, ever, ever
sit on the back porch
and swap ghost stories
over steaming coffee mugs

ever, ever, ever again.

Her death was not her end.

Grief is cold fingers
tapping on my window
at night.

Keeping me awake.
Keeping me aware.

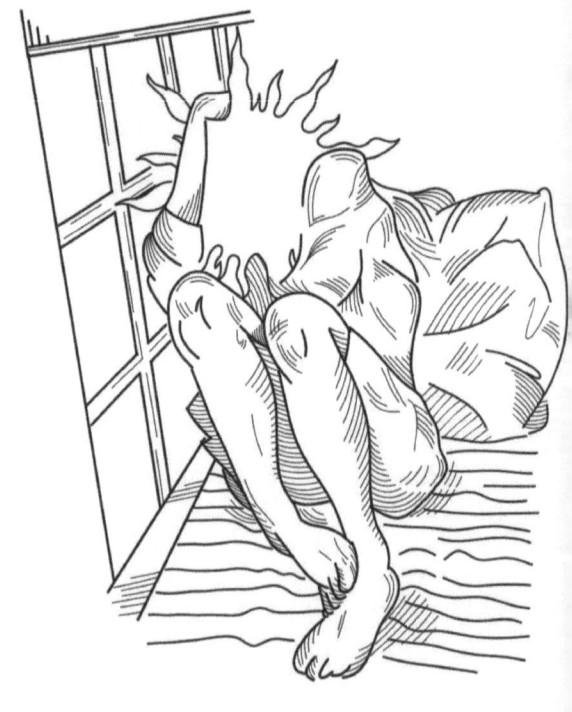

Guilt, like grief,
manifests in
strange ways.

I don't know why
I want to die.

(I do, I do, I do.)

All my grief says
the same thing-
this isn't how
it's supposed to be.

The world laughs,
holds my hope by my throat,
says: but this is how it is.

You tell your sadness,
"in a sharp set of knives,
I looked for a hand to hold.

I could not stop myself
from needing to belong somewhere,
even if that somewhere
was a burial ground."

She says,
"we were put on this earth
desperate, hungry, and
willing.

what made you think it
would end differently?"

So you're telling me
I will have this chest rot
until I die?

I began to dream
while awake
and soon enough

I couldn't tell you
what was real
and what wasn't.

- You are here with me.

Everything I write
is a cry for help
but what will I say
when they'll reach my door step?

Save me from me.

What's the very worst?

Being offered water
when you're drowning?

Or living by an ocean
and dying of thirst?

Regardless,
I have done both.
I have lived both.

It's
12:55 pm
and all that haunts me
are my words.
They crawl out
from under my bed
and infest me.
They bite
and they screech
and they won't let me be.

I said "goodnight"
but it sounded more like "goodbye".

Hearts
don't shatter
they rot.

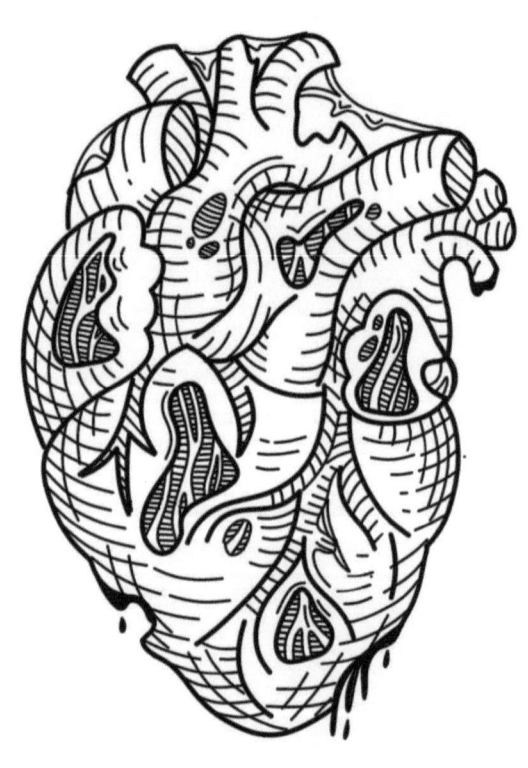

I could be
ninety-nine percent sure
that everything is fine,
but it's that
one percent of doubt
that drives me insane.

It's why,
for my whole life,
I've gotten up
once everyone
has fallen asleep
just to check,
to make sure,
that everyone I love
is still breathing.

This is me,
palms open,
face up,
asking for saving.

This is me,
blue lips,
bare skin,
screaming in silence.

This is me,
no brick in hand,
no more wars
left to fight.

This is me,
hand on heart.

This is me,
I am here.
I am all that's left.

This is me,
missing you.

At least,
in my poems
I can stay
with you.

I believe
there will always be
a place in my heart
that still hurts
whenever I think of you.

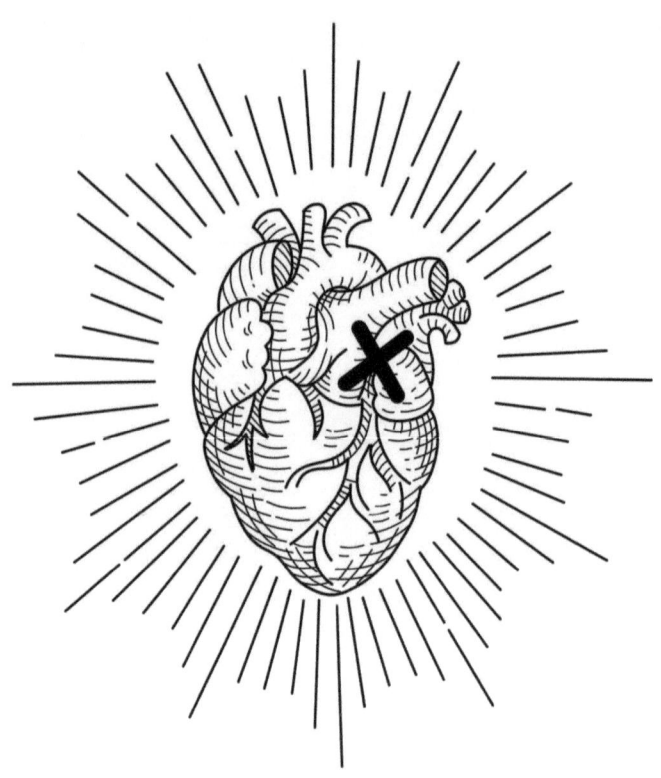

Since you left
I got worse at baking
but I can drink coffee black
without making a face.

I learned that it's possible
to not kill plants
and that I look best
in the mornings
wearing forest green.

I've figured out how
to ask for what I want
and to yell
when I'm being talked over.

That I can make people
feel things they've been ignoring
just by being honest.

If I'm being honest
I still let myself
think of you
once a day

and I will keep asking
even if you never hear me.

Can you let go of someone
without forgetting how they made you feel?

For now,
I'll think about it most of the time
and forget about it long enough
to be happy every now and then.

It won't always be this way,
but for now, it is this way
and I have to learn
how to be okay with that.

You have a few more
heavy steps to walk
but tomorrow,

tomorrow
you'll find someone new
and someone new will find you.

I didn't know
you existed
six weeks ago

but now you're
writing me letters,
kissing my forehead,
buying me trinkets,
calling me honeybee,
singing my favourite songs.

If you keep this up
I might start to think
that being with you
is better than being alone.

You brought the needle
and I brought the thread.

We meant to mend our
two broken hearts,
but we ended up
stitching them together.

Somehow,
my soul knew
your soul
before we
ever had the chance
to meet.

- It was like coming home
after a long, long day.

If he was
my cup of tea,
then you are
my cup of coffee.

Tea simply isn't enough
for me sometimes,
but coffee
can get me
through anything.

The world needs you.

It needs your kindness.
Your grace.
Your light.

It needs your story.
It needs your lessons.
It needs your journey.

You may not need the world,
but it needs you.

I need
your lazy,
coffee-drinking mornings.

I need
your famous pancakes.

I need
your pumpkin-picking afternoons.

I need
your footsteps following me
as I browse the bookstore again.

I need
your clothes strewn
all over my our floor.

I need
your sidelong looks
only I understand.

I need
your comfortably quiet
midnight moments.

I need all of it.

I don't wanna grow old with someone.

I wanna finger paint with someone
when were forty.

Play with each other's hair
when we're fifty.

Make smiley face pancakes
when we're sixty.

Sock puppets
when we're sixty-seven.

Spin in the rain
when we're seventy.

Jump in puddles
when were seventy-two.

Make pillow forts
when we're eighty.

Play make-believe
when we're ninety.

I wanna grow young with someone.
I wanna grow young with you.

You rewrote
all my old poems
erased the hurt.

Made me feel like love
was always this easy
and now everything
I've ever written
is about you.

Everything I've ever
written is about you

It only takes a second or two
to look into their eyes
and decide whether
you're home or at just another
perfectly decorated house.

I like to pretend that I know
we will end up together.

Drinking coffee
from the same chipped mug,
our lips cutting
on exposed porcelain.

I imagine we kiss
to ease the pain.
and we laugh.
oh, we laugh.

I can't promise
how I will feel
tomorrow but
tonight I am
in love with you.

Falling in love is cloud nine,
dancing in your underwear,
good morning texts and
giving someone the ability
to make you cry.

I will take down
these walls for you
if you promise
to build a home in me.

Plant your garden
in the cracks of my skin
mud, gravel, everything.

Let my blood be water
to cater to your needs.

Terrible, terrible human,
thinks that barbarity
and love share the same meaning.

I want to build a house
with your breath.

Paint the walls
with your tongue.

Make a string of lights
with your teeth.

Lay the foundation
with the feeling I get
when you say my name.

Your words are like bricks.

I am going to understand
what love is.

It's an act of service.

What I am trying to say is,
your dishwasher is empty,
and the thing is,

I love you.

I wonder if
I'm the first person
you called sunshine
or kissed three times.
Is this new to you too
or is this a deja vu?

If only you could see yourself
from my eyes.

You wouldn't see the darkness.
You wouldn't see the despair.
You wouldn't see the coldness.

That you feel.

You would see the light.
You would see the joy.
You would see the warmth.

That you bring to my life.

Every time we see each other,
you leave landmarks in my head,
little vacation spots for me to visit
whenever I'm feeling alone.

I love you
like I have grown old
with you already.

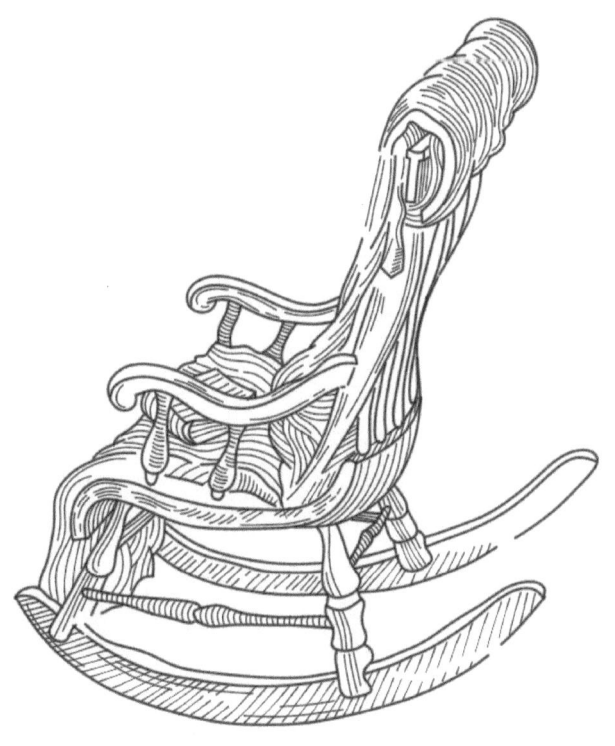

My biggest fear is
that I will end up
telling you everything
that keeps me
up at night.

That you will store
this information away
and book a one way flight

while I wait with
trembling hands
to see if you'll ever
come back to me.

Baby,
I've peeled off my skin for you.
I'm ripping away muscle.

Give me a moment
to crack open my rib cage.
I have no use for
these bones anymore.

Excuse me while
I cut through veins,
sever arteries.

I think I've almost got it.

Now it's pulsing in my palm here,
take my heart it's better off with you.

There were days
when I wanted you to feel
the warmth of a home
so badly
that if you had asked me
to burn my bones to ashes
to build a fire for you
I would have.

It feels as if I am
standing with glass
walls all around me.

The wall behind me
keeps me from touching
all that I have touched.

The wall in front of me
keeps me from touching
all that I could touch.

The walls beside me
keep me from feeling
anything around me.

The wall above me
is there just to keep
me from escaping.

- I'm in love,
but I can't feel your skin.

How many times in the average day
do you think of me while you're with her
and brush the thought away?

I feel prettier
in the sun.

I need nose freckles
to feel like myself.

Hold my hand
before it melts.

Tell me I'm prettier
when it's warmer.

Tell me I'm prettier
than her.

I have turned myself
inside out loving you-
hoping that if my heart sit
on the outside of my body,
perhaps you may
take more notice of it.

Where is she
while you're with me?

Where is she
while you're with me?

Where is she
while you're with me?

Is this what you wanted?

I'm sorry
you were afraid
of my kind of love.

How many times
will I let myself be
a second choice
before I learn?

I tried so hard
to be whole for you
but it turns out
you like me better
when I'm in pieces.

I am in love with you,
and I have no say in it.

It happens, it happens,
and it keeps on happening.

And I sometimes find myself
wondering if maybe, just maybe,
I had a little bit of control over this,
would I still stay here?

Would I knowingly choose
these lingering, never-ending
explosions in my chest, or
would I choose the silence
of never having loved?

Every time,
I choose the explosions,
the violent displays
of heaven having once
lived in my chest.

I choose to feel.
I choose to be alive.

He loves me.
He loves me not.

He loves her.
He loves her not.

He loves me.
He loves me not.

He loves her.
He loves her not.

He loves me.
He loves me not.

He loves her.
He loves her not.

He loves me.
He loves me not.

He loves her.

- I ran out of petals.

Our teeth sparkled
bright white when
we first met
but you drank too much red wine
and I too much black coffee.

So now these stains
on what used to be
pure white
are all that's left of us.

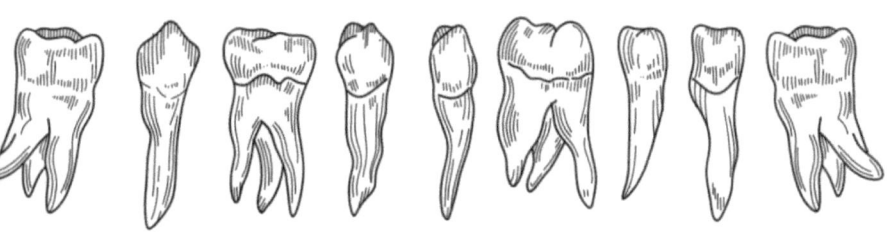

We were always almost perfect,
right there on the edge of it,
so close we could almost touch it.

And I don't think either of us
truly wanted the torture
of spending even just one more day
being a stone's throw away
from happiness.

- A heartbreaking almost.

When it finally
came time for him
to leave,
he packed up
all my poetry
in a suitcase
and took it with him.

- First my heart, then my words.

If I were to see you now
I'm not even sure
how I will react
is it strange that
I just crave for your
presence without
an actual reason?

You stopped saying goodnight
and I stopped sleeping.

He may have felt like home
but he'll never
keep you warm at night.

You've made your decision
and you wanted me
to be okay with it.

Please, I said,
it can't end like this.
I spent the last few months
believing that you were
the person for me.

I can't,
you said.

That was the last time
we ever spoke on the phone.

We could have been
anything in this world
but you chose
to leave.

I don't know where you are;
it's so hard to reach you these days.
But if I had the chance
to tell you just one thing,

I'd say,
the last time we spoke,
we were angry at each other;
I hope that's not how
you remember us.

Two days later
after you left,
12:22pm,
sitting in a cafe,
had my coffee
but I couldn't drink it
all I did was saying
I'm sorry
to myself
over and over again.

It's only now I realise
how differently we handled our break up.

While you replaced my body
with someone else's.

I tried to replicate what we had.

You wrapped yourself
around another person.

I collected every part of you
I still had and stuck it to someone else.

I fell in love and I hope
it would make me fall
out of love with you

It didn't
but I tried anyway and I cried
and held myself and stopped eating.

I was so desperate for us
to come back together.

You just wanted
another pair of legs to be between.

I wanted nothing
to be between us.

I would rather
feel my soul split in half
from the long nights
of wishing you were with me,
than hold close someone
who will never have my heart
the way that you do.

You were awful to me,
but nostalgia has since
made you beautiful.

We were okay before,
We will be okay after.

I knew I would be okay.

I would be okay because
I was whole before you.

I breathed.
I smiled.
I laughed.
I cried.
I felt.

During you,
I was still a whole person.

I breathed.
I smiled.
I laughed.
I cried.
I felt.

After you,
I was still a whole person.

I just had trouble breathing.
I just had trouble smiling.
I just had trouble laughing.
I cried too hard
and felt even harder.

Let your pain
hold the hands,
point at your scars
and tell you,

"this.. this is
from where
the light comes in."

I spent a long time wondering
if I was too much.

If people hurting me
meant more about me
than it did about them.

I spent a long time
convincing myself
that the reason people left
was because of me.

That I simply
wasn't good enough.

I spent a long time thinking
I was at fault.

Apologizing when I loved too much.
Apologizing when I cared too much.
Apologizing when people left.

It was all me.
It was never me.

It is not your responsibility
to save everyone.

Don't put that kind of
pressure on yourself.

Do the best you can
to spread your light
where you can.

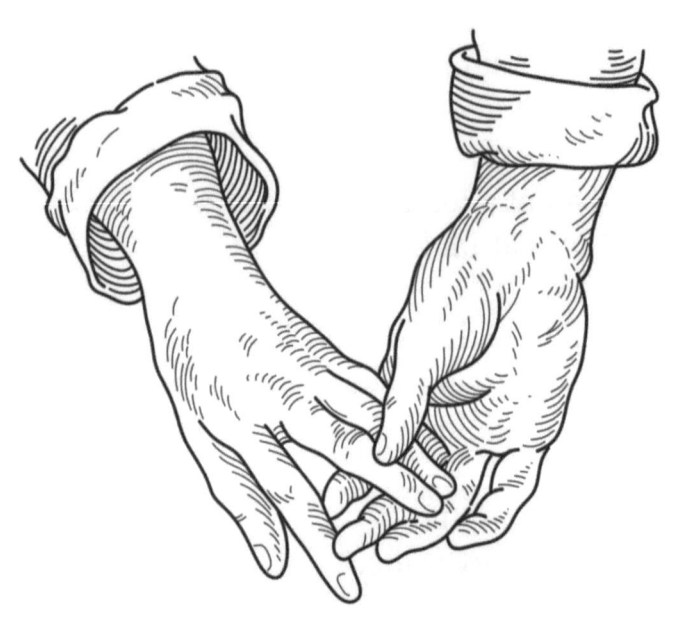

The pain will settle in,
burrow into your chest
and make itself a home there.

And you won't know
what to do with it for a while,
but you'll hold on anyways,
because there's always hope that,
someday, maybe you will.

I'm choosing to look
at us ending
as the start of something.

And though
I'm only one step
out of our grave,
the view is already beautiful.

They say healing takes time,
that time heals all wounds,
so I wait, I wait, and I wait.

And while every clock I see
ticks ahead like I know them to,
time has stalled in my head.

I am still right back there,
right in your arms
with everything
feeling right in the world.

So tell me, what good is time if
nothing ever changes in me?

I'm beginning to think
that time heals nothing,
but that we can eventually
heal ourselves if we are
given enough time.

I had a dream
where I spoke
to my past,
and it said,
"I'm still here
because you
allow it."

Did I heal?
Or did I force
myself to forget?

I think I lost a few years
on my life
worrying about
the future.
Maybe I can gain
a few back by
forgiving.
the past.

Unlike love and pain,
healing is a choice.

Choose it.

Last night,
I had an epiphany of the heart, a sudden
realization that everything will be okay.

- And so it will be.

Remember this:
You deserve peace.

When I look at you, I see;

I see grief was your only comfort.
I see neglect was your only warmth.
I see pain was your only pleasure.

When I look in the mirror,
I no longer see you.

I see me.
I broke the cycle.

I knew I was healing,
when loud footsteps on stairs
no longer made me jump.

I knew I was healing,
when crying wasn't only
a sign of sadness.

I knew I was healing,
when I missed the sun
on rainy days.

I knew I was healing,
when the distance between us grew,
and I didn't feel guilty for letting it.

When neglect was replaced with love.
When grief was replaced with comfort.
When a house was replaced with a home.

I found the strength to be again.

"What comes next?"
once was a question
that used to haunt me,
but now, it's a question
that fills my heart with hope.

She said,
I'll always find a way to shine.
I belong to the sun.

© 2024 Laira Schmitt
Publisher: BoD · Books on Demand GmbH,
In de Tarpen 42, 22848 Norderstedt
Printed by: Libri Plureos GmbH,
Friedensallee 273, 22763 Hamburg
ISBN: 978-3-7583-0393-7